SERGEI
RACHMANINOV

SONATA

FOR

VIOLONCELLO AND PIANO

G MINOR

OP. 19

MUSIC MINUS ONE

mmo
3731

Suggestions for using this MMO edition

WE HAVE TRIED to create a product that will provide you an easy way to learn and perform this sonata with a full accompaniment in the comfort of your own home. Because it involves a fixed performance, there is an inherent lack of flexibility in tempo and cadenza length. The following MMO features and techniques will reduce these inflexibilities and help you maximize the effectiveness of the MMO practice and performance system:

Where the soloist begins a movement solo, we have provided an introductory measure with subtle taps inserted at the actual tempo before the soloist's entrance. Track-breaks on your CD are conveniently located throughout the piece at the beginnings of practice sections, and are cross-referenced in the score. This should help you quickly find a desired place in the music as you learn the piece.

Regarding tempi: we have observed generally accepted tempi, but some may wish to perform at a different tempo, or to slow down or speed up the accompaniment for practice purposes. You can purchase from MMO specialized CD players and recorders which allow variable speed while maintaining proper pitch. This is an indispensable tool for the serious musician and you may wish to look into purchasing this useful piece of equipment for full enjoyment of all your MMO editions.

We want to provide you with the most useful practice and performance accompaniments possible. If you have any suggestions for improving the MMO system, please feel free to contact us. You can reach us by e-mail at *info@musicminusone.com*.

A NOTE FROM THE EDITOR

FOR THE 'CELLIST, playing with a duo partner in the form of a pre-recorded and inflexible piano track will present many challenges. On one hand it will help you greatly to become familiar with the work, but on the other hand, as you get to know the piece better and better you will develop your own uniquely personal interpretation. The final stage of learning this great work will be one where you free yourself from the interpretation we are presenting you with and find tempi, colors and expressive nuances that will be uniquely your own. This recording will be invaluable to you in the beginning stages as you learn the piece.

Sections where there are tempo changes will probably present the biggest challenges. I would suggest that you obtain a copy of the full score (or smaller study edition) and listen to our performance while reading it so you can clearly see how the 'cello and piano fit together, paying special attention to tempo changes. When you

have a reasonable command over the 'cello part and know the piece by ear fairly well, start playing along with the solo piano version. If the tempo-changes continue to be problematic I would suggest listening to the solo piano track while looking at the full score and becoming very aware of how the 'cello part fits in and at what rate the tempo changes.

The Rachmaninov sonata for cello and piano is, for the 'cellist, what I consider to be a "sound piece." By this, I mean that pure beauty and lushness of tone is of paramount importance. Rachmaninov is skillfully tapping the violoncello's ability to produce a gorgeous, singing line through his use of lush and heartfelt melodies. The 'cellist's ability to produce a warm *vibrato* and a seamless but beautifully sculpted *legato* line can be greatly enhanced by work on this piece.

My hope for those using this recording is that it be a great tool to accelerate the learning process and ultimately support personal creativity and fulfillment.

—*Nancy Green*

Music Minus One

3731

CONTENTS

SERGEI RACHMANINOV

SERGEI RACHMANINOV was born at Oneg, in Novgorod, Russia, on 1 April, 1873, son of a captain of the Imperial Guards, and a talented, well-to-do mother. He might have followed in his father's footsteps if a series of adverse circumstances had not depleted the family's income and holdings.

When Sergei was nine, his parents separated, and he and his mother went to live in St. Petersburg. He entered the St. Petersburg College of Music, where his superior talents enabled him to coast along without applying himself to his studies with any particular diligence. In 1885, however, Nikolai Zverev at the Moscow Conservatory became Rachmaninov's teacher and guiding spirit, taking him into his home and giving him direction and incentive.

Rachmaninov became a brilliant pianist, winning in 1891 the highest honors for the instrument. He met his idol, Tchaikovsky, and studied composition under Arensky. For his final examination at the Conservatory, he composed the one-act opera *Aleko*, based on Pushkin's poem *The Gypsies*, in two weeks! At 20, he wrote his famous Prelude in C-sharp minor for piano, which was first performed in London by his cousin Alexander Siloti, and was a fantastic success.

This amazing triumph was, however, much tempered by the unexpected failure of his First Symphony, op. 13— a work that strongly showed the influence of Tchaikovsky. Although it was premiered in St. Petersburg under the most auspicious circumstances, with Glazunov conducting, its reception was abominably scathing. Cesar Cui wrote: "if there were a conservatory in Hell, Rachmaninov would get first prize for his symphony, so devilish are the discords he places before us."

This failure was crushing and, for a brief period, Rachmaninov became assistant conductor at a Moscow opera house, perfecting his conducting skills. In 1898, he conducted and played in London, but his successes there did not pull him out of a lengthy period of despair and creative paralysis.

What exacerbated matters was that, after the First Symphony's failure, the young Rachmaninov simply failed to "get back on the horse again." Instead, he began devoting himself to conducting, particularly operas. He found he was gifted at this, too, and due to his nascent friendship with the great basso Feodor Chaliapin, he enjoyed conducting enormously. But this happiness didn't last for long. In his role as composer, try as he may to create greater and more complex works, he found himself stymied.

Family and friends set up two meetings between Rachmaninov and the greatest living Russian writer and religious-thinker: Count Leo Tolstoy. But help from the aged, great author of *War and Peace* and *Anna Karenina* was not forthcoming. At their first meeting, Tolstoy stated to Rachmaninov: "You must work. Do you think that I am pleased with myself? Work. I must work every day." Rachmaninov knew this, but he couldn't break through the invisible barrier that was holding him back. At his second visit with the author, Tolstoy asked Rachmaninov to play some of his music for him. Rachmaninov did so, after which Tolstoy looked the troubled young composer straight in the eye, and asked him: "Tell me, does anyone want this type of music?"

Ultra-sensitive man that Rachmaninov was, these meetings with Tolstoy only served to demoralize him further. Sensing his ever-increasing despair, some of Rachmaninov's relatives sent him to a family friend, Dr. Nikolai Dahl, a specialist in neurology and hypnosis. Fortuitously, this doctor was an amateur musician with a keen understanding of music, and, more importantly, appreciated Rachmaninov's work as well.

This was in 1900, the year of Freud's revolutionary *Interpretation of Dreams*. What Dr. Dahl practiced upon the young composer several days a week for several months was a form of early psychoanalytic hypnosis. Over and over the good doctor repeated to the half-asleep Rachmaninov the suggestive phrases "You will begin to write your concerto…it will be excellent…you will work with great facility…." When Rachmaninov subsequently went on a tour with Chaliapin to Italy, his block simply vanished. He began composing prolifically, climaxing this trip with the writing of the detailed sketches of what became the Second Concerto.

In 1901 came the premiere of that enormously successful concerto, and with this began a great and fruitful period in Rachmaninov's life. Later that year he completed the enduring Violoncello Sonata, op. 19, which in texture and melodic style draws heavily on the piano concerto which immediately preceded it. In 1902 he married and in 1903 was busy at work as opera composer and conductor at the Imperial Grand Theater. Two operas were completed and produced: *The Miser Knight*, based on Pushkin and *Francesca da Rimini*, on a libretto by Tchaikovsky's brother, Modest. In 1906 Rachmaninov took his wife and baby daughter to Dresden after refusing, with typical lack of self-confidence, an offer of a concert tour of America. He wrote a friend: "You could not possibly understand what tortures I live through when I realize that the question has to be decided by me alone. The trouble is that I am incapable of making any decision by myself. My hands tremble!"

Dresden proved to be a creatively stimulating city for Rachmaninov, and he composed several large works there: the Second Symphony; the symphonic poem *Isle of the Dead*; and the First Piano Sonata. Returning to Ivanovka, his cherished family country estate, in the summer of 1909, he composed the thrilling and colorful Third Piano Concerto in preparation for the American concert tour which he finally accepted for the 1909-1910 season. In the United States, Rachmaninov was acclaimed as composer, conductor and pianist, and was offered the post of conductor of the Boston Symphony. He returned, instead, to Russia and became a powerful figure on the musical scene as conductor of the Moscow Philharmonic. A rival faction led by Serge Koussevitsky appeared, and there soon raged a heated battle between this champion of the new, modern Russian composers and the more conservative Rachmaninov.

In 1913, tired of conducting, Rachmaninov went with his family to Switzerland and then to Rome, where he found the incentive to compose his choral symphony *The Bells*, inspired by Edgar Allen Poe's immortal poem. It is scored for large orchestra, mixed chorus and three solo voices. Each of its four movements suggests a different bell tone and evokes a distinct mood: the *allegro*—sleigh bells; the *lento*—golden wedding bells; the *scherzo*—alarm bells; and the *lento lugubre*—tolling iron bells.

In 1917, as the dangers of the Russian Revolution increased around him, Rachmaninov, an aristocrat from a land-owning family, feared for the safety of his family. Fortunately, the offer of a Scandinavian concert tour provided an excuse to leave the country. Carrying only a few personal belongings, they left Russia in a blizzard. A year later, on 10 November 1918, they came to America. Rachmaninov decided to concentrate on the piano. This was a felicitous decision—during his long virtuoso career, he was acclaimed as one of the foremost pianists of his times.

Rachmaninov made many recordings of his work with Leopold Stokowski and the Philadelphia Orchestra. He lived in New York, practiced and concertized in the winters, relaxed in his summer home in Switzerland, finally moving to Beverly Hills, where he enjoyed gardening in the congenial California climate. He composed very little, but in 1934 he wrote and performed the *Rhapsody on a Theme of Paganini* for piano and orchestra. Its success was dazzling. It has a vitality unencumbered by his former brooding romanticism, indicating that Rachmaninov was aware at last of the new age in music. The Eighteenth Variation of the *Rhapsody* has become a popular favorite.

Regarding Rachmaninov's particular approach to composing, he wrote:

"I am not a composer who produces works to the formulas of preconceived theories. Music, I have always felt, should be the expression of a composer's complex personality; it should not be arrived at cerebrally, tailor-made to fit certain specifications. Too much radical music is sheer sham, because the composer has set about revolutionizing the laws of music before he has even mastered them himself... In my composition, I am greatly helped if I have in mind a book I have recently read, or a beautiful picture, or a poem. Sometimes I keep in mind a definite story, which I try to convert into themes without ever disclosing the source of my inspiration, for I am not writing program music. This is particularly true when I write one of my shorter pieces for the piano. A short piece has always given me more pain, and has presented to me many more problems than a symphony or a concerto....I compose because I must give expression to my feelings, just as I talk because I must give utterance to my thoughts."

Despite a sometimes very painful struggle with cancer, Rachmaninov played with strength and authority until the very end. It was during a concert tour early in 1943, when he was close to 70, that he was taken ill and brought to his home at 610 N. Elm Drive, Beverly Hills. He died there on 28 March, and was buried in Kensico Cemetery in New York.

To A. Brandukov

SONATA
for Violoncello and Piano

Edited by Nancy Green

Sergei Rachmaninov
(1873-1943)
op. 19

1) Two-finger fifth.

2) It is nearly impossible to get a clean C *arco* on beat three as well as a clean B *pizz.* on beat four. I would suggest keeping the bow-hand in *arco* position, but with 2nd finger extended for the *pizz.*

3) The octaves are best plucked on a sweep from right to left with thumb.

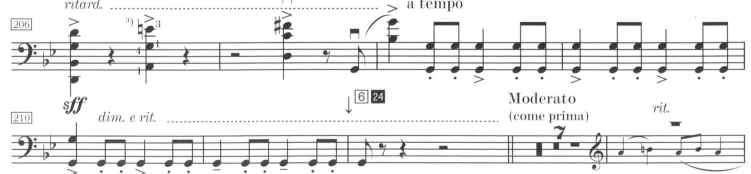

1) From here until the *a tempo* at bar 229 is perhaps the most difficult passage in the entire piece for 'cello projection due to the heavy piano writing. I would recommend frequent bow changes. (Before a performance, this is a good passage to test balance.)

2) This fingering works well if you are comfortable with two-finger fifths.

3) Due to the unplayable stretch required here I recommend first playing the G+A together with 4+1, then shifting as you break the chord and playing the G+E together with 3+1. One could also play low A with thumb + the other notes with 3+1.

II

MMO 3731

1 measure of taps (4 taps) precedes music

Allegro scherzando (♩. =88)

1) To facilitate a quick preparation for the *arco*, *pizz.* from left to right holding bow in *arco* position and extending the 2nd finger

Un poco meno mosso

Tempo I

12

¹) In order to be audible here in *fortissimo* one can sneak in an extra up-bow.
In live performance this will be inaudible. (In a recording it is to be avoided!)

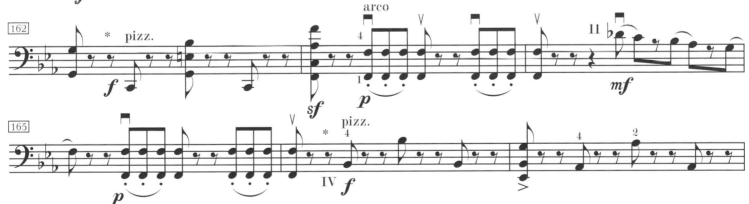

14

Un poco meno mosso

Tempo I

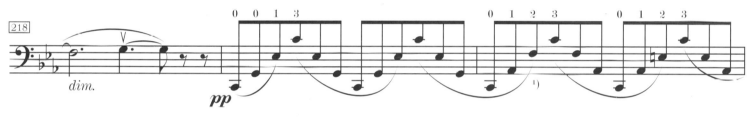

¹) Two-finger fifth.
²) + Left-hand *pizz.*

III

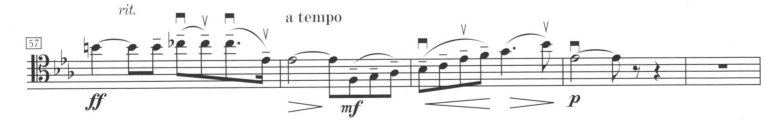

¹) At tip of bow

MMO 3731

18

IV

¹) Two bowing options: one above, one below

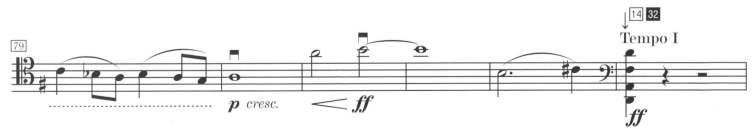

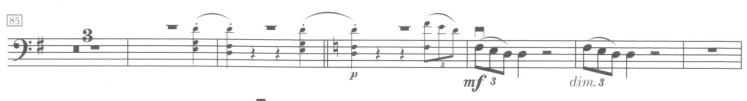

1) Two-finger fifth.
2) This note can be doubled with open A string.

¹) Two-finger fifth.

Engraving: Wieslaw Novak

MMO 3731

MUSIC MINUS ONE
50 Executive Boulevard
Elmsford, New York 10523-1325
800-669-7464 (U.S.)/914-592-1188 (International)

www.musicminusone.com
e-mail: info@musicminusone.com

MMO 3731   Pub. No. 00345   Printed in Canada